Face to Face

SPANIARDS & AZTECS

Fiona Macdonald

SIMON & SCHUSTER
YOUNG BOOKS

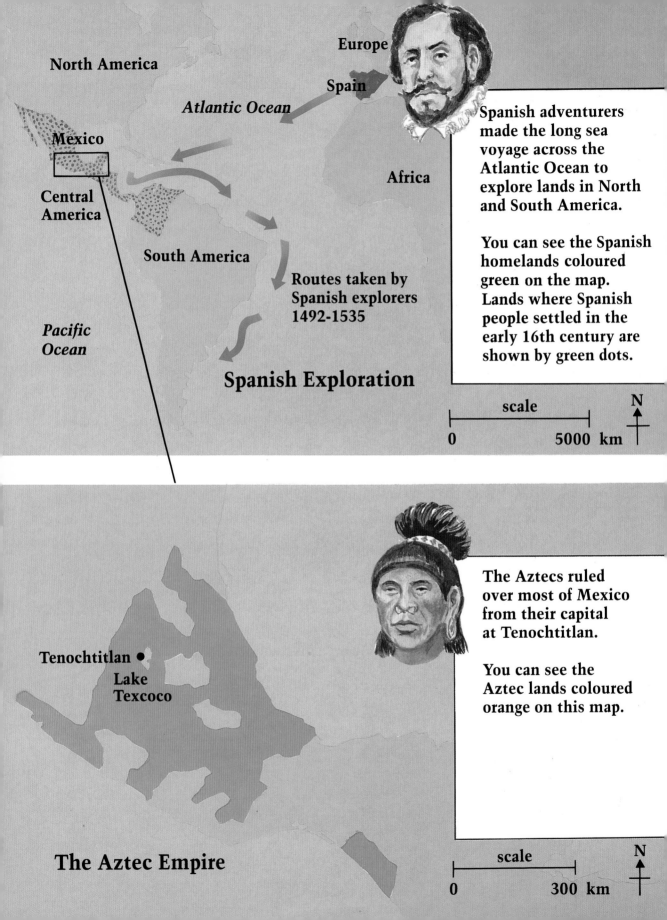

North America

Europe

Spain

Atlantic Ocean

Mexico

Africa

Central
America

South America

*Pacific
Ocean*

Routes taken by
Spanish explorers
1492-1535

Spanish Exploration

Spanish adventurers
made the long sea
voyage across the
Atlantic Ocean to
explore lands in North
and South America.

You can see the Spanish
homelands coloured
green on the map.
Lands where Spanish
people settled in the
early 16th century are
shown by green dots.

scale

N

0   5000 km

Tenochtitlan
Lake
Texcoco

The Aztecs ruled
over most of Mexico
from their capital
at Tenochtitlan.

You can see the
Aztec lands coloured
orange on this map.

The Aztec Empire

scale

N

0   300 km

Contents

Who were the Aztecs?

The Aztecs lived in Mexico, a harsh land in central America. They settled there around AD 1300, after a long journey from their original homeland.
The Aztecs left their old home because the climate changed. There was no rain for many years.
Crops died in the fields, and they faced starvation.

When the Aztecs reached Mexico, they settled on the shores of a great lake in the central valley of Mexico. They built a city, called Tenochtitlan, on an island in the middle of this lake. Soon, they conquered all the peoples living nearby, and ruled over a rich and powerful empire.

An Aztec mother and child. These figures were made by Aztec craft workers, probably around 1450. The mother has arranged her hair in a typical Aztec style, with plaits looped above her head to make two 'horns'.

Cactus growing in the dry, mountainous land where the Aztecs lived.
Fruits of the smaller cactus, called the 'prickly pear', were sold in Aztec markets. They contained sweet refreshing juice.

RVFO
N LEP TO.

EL L^DO XPTOBAL MOSQVERA.
D FIGVEROA. AVDITOR GRAL.

EL ALM^TE M^QVES D
QVVENDO DEL O. D SANT^GO
G^RAL D LA ESQ^DRA D CAN-
TABRIA.

HOSP
ARMAS NON ARRVIS OBSTA

Spanish soldiers, dressed in 16th century clothes and armour, shown on a picture made out of painted ceramic tiles. Some of the soldiers are carrying guns. These were a fairly new invention at that time.

Who were the Spanish?

The Spanish people lived in Spain, a country in southern Europe. They had been settled there for thousands of years. Around AD 1450, when the Aztecs were taking control of Mexico, Spain was a wealthy land. Farmers grew crops of wheat, grapes and oranges, and raised sheep for meat and for fine, silky wool. Craft workers made beautiful carvings and mosaics. Spanish scholars were famous throughout Europe.

But this wealth and achievement was not shared equally. Although a few great families were rich, many peasants were poor. Even some nobles found it hard to live. They began to look for new ways of making a fortune.

Spanish noble families lived in grand palaces like these, with strong stone walls, cool courtyards and many rooms, Ordinary people lived in smaller, simpler homes.

Aztec lifestyle

Mexico is a harsh environment. The land is rocky and mountainous. Not many crops will grow there. It is hot during the day, but bitterly cold at night.

But the Aztecs found ways to survive. They grew vegetables in gardens all round the shores of their island city, made out of fertile mud dug from the bottom of the lake. They planted maize and cactus on the dry mountain slopes. They ate fish, frogs and snails from the lake, as well as edible dogs, which they reared in their homes. For shelter, they built houses from mud bricks and roofed them with straw. To keep warm, they made cloaks and skirts from cactus fibres, and decorated them with embroidery.

The Aztecs worshipped friendly local gods, as well as the terrifying gods of sun and rain. These statues of gods and goddesses who protected families and helped the crops to grow were made for an Aztec household shrine.

The city of Tenochtitlan was built on an island in a lake. The Aztecs built gardens all around the lake shores by laying branches and grass mats in the shallow water then covering them with mud, dug from the bottom of the lake. They grew good crops of maize, fruit and vegetables on this new land.

Lake Texcoco

Aztec house

chillies

peppers

tomatoes

potatoes

bundle of dry grass

Aztec farmer

maize

The power of the gods

The Aztecs believed that the gods ruled their world. There were many gods and goddesses, each with different powers. The most important were Huitzilopoctli, the sun-god, and Tlaloc, the god who brought rain. Aztec emperors built a great temple to worship them in the centre of their city. They also feared Quetzalcoatl, a mysterious, ancient god.

The Aztecs thought that these gods had to be fed with human blood, or else the world would come to an end. So they fought with neighbouring peoples, and captured as many as they could. Then they killed these captives and offered their hearts and blood as food for the gods.

This mask of the god Texcetlipoca was made to look like a real human skull. It is decorated with a blue precious stone called turquoise, and with a black shiny stone, called obsidian, that is produced when a volcano erupts.

The great pyramid of Chichen Itza,
a city to the south of the Aztec capital
of Tenochtitlan. It was built by the Maya
peoples, who lived in Mexico before the
Aztecs arrived. The Aztecs and other
Mexican peoples made sacrifices to
the god Queztalcoatl here.

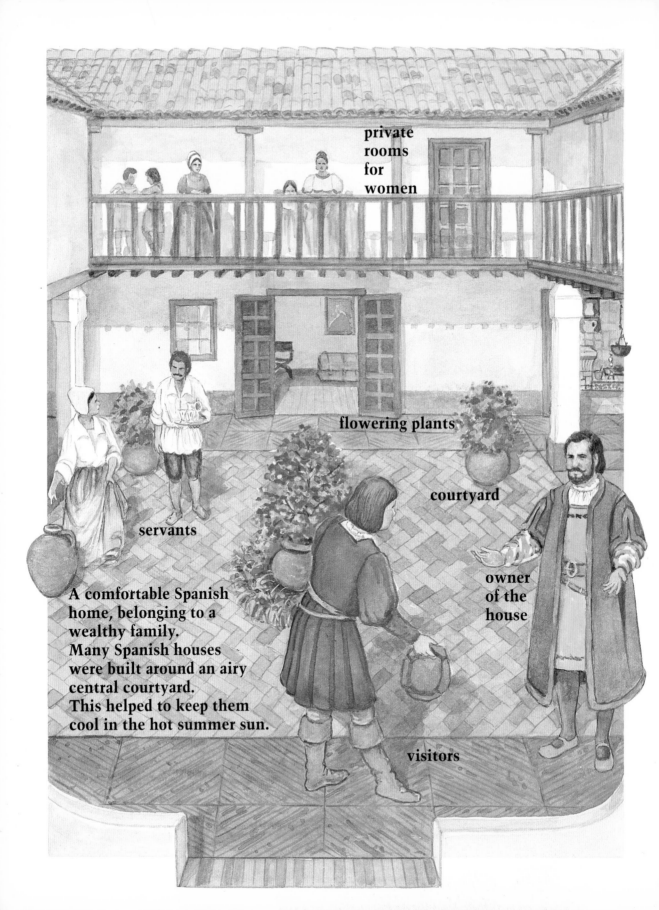

private
rooms
for
women

flowering plants

courtyard

servants

owner
of the
house

A comfortable Spanish
home, belonging to a
wealthy family.
Many Spanish houses
were built around an airy
central courtyard.
This helped to keep them
cool in the hot summer sun.

visitors

Spanish lifestyle

Spain was ruled by kings and queens. They governed with the help of leading noblemen who owned large estates. Ordinary people worked as labourers on these estates, and in their own fields. Other men and women made a living in markets and workshops in the towns.

There was another great power in Spain—the Roman Catholic Church. Priests and church leaders preached the Christian faith, telling ordinary people how to live. They ran hospitals, schools and universities. Church administrators, lawyers and scholars also helped Spanish kings and queens to rule.

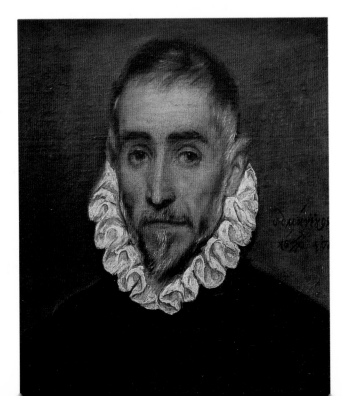

Portrait of a Spanish nobleman who lived in the 16th century. Spain was ruled by men like him.

15

The search for gold

Some Spanish people made their living from the sea.
They caught fish, made salt, and carried cargo.
These Spanish sailors were adventurous.
After about 1400, they travelled south, to the
West African coast, and westward, to the Atlantic
islands called the Azores.

In 1492, Christopher Columbus, an Italian explorer
supported by the Spanish king and queen, also
sailed westward. He hoped to travel right round
the world to reach the East Indies, famous for gold
and jewels. In fact, he landed in the Bahama Islands,
close to America. When he got back to Spain,
he told about the rich 'New World'. Soon, other
Spanish adventurers sailed west, in search of gold.

When he arrived in America,
Columbus thought the local
people were 'savages'.
Today, we know that they
were skilled at many crafts
and occupations. These scenes
of daily life come from a codex
made by Aztec scribes.

16

American coast

Spanish ships

look-out

sail

mast

For the Spaniards, America was an exciting 'New World'. Columbus and his men sailed there hoping to find adventure and rich treasures. They did not consider how their actions might harm the people already living there.

The end of the world?

By around 1500, not long after Columbus reached America, the Aztec empire was at its most powerful. Tenochtitlan was now a large, rich and beautiful city. The Aztec emperors ruled over a mighty empire, and received splendid tributes of food, clothes, gold, weapons and jewellery from all the people they had conquered.

But this was not to last for very long. In 1519, emperor Moctezuma received reports of strange 'floating houses' and fearsome 'monsters' arriving on the Mexican coast. This news reminded him of the old prophecy that one day, the fierce god Queztalcoatl would come back to Mexico. Then the world would end, in fire and floods.

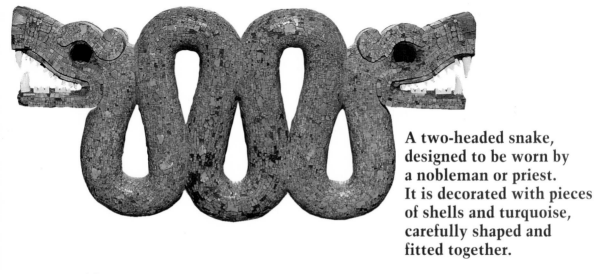

A two-headed snake, designed to be worn by a nobleman or priest. It is decorated with pieces of shells and turquoise, carefully shaped and fitted together.

This finely-carved stone stood by the great temples in the heart of Tenochtitlan. It records the complicated Aztec calendar system. Aztec priests measured time by observing the movements of the sun, moon and stars. They were skilful astronomers.

Aztec scribes recorded important events in documents known as codexes. They used pictures and symbols to describe what had happened. Codexes also record Aztec religious beliefs. These pictures show the sun-god (top) and the god of darkness (bottom) standing outside their temples.

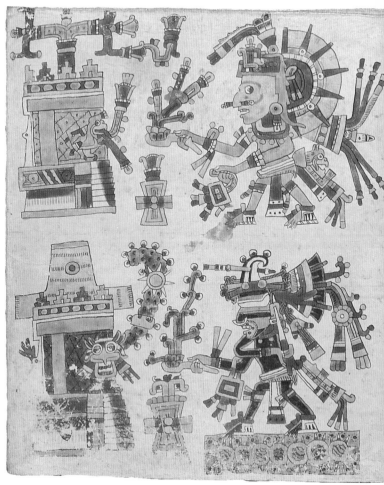

The Spanish arrive

In 1519, a Spanish nobleman named Hernan Cortes arrived in America. He was poor, brave, skilful, greedy, and very ambitious. He wanted to find gold and become rich. He studied the reports sent back by other travellers, and decided to land in Mexico.

Moctezuma sent a group of nobles to meet Cortes and his troops. He still believed that Cortes might be a god. So he told the nobles to offer him rich gifts, and then ask him to leave the Aztec lands. But Cortes refused. Helped by enemies of the Aztecs, and guided by a captured Mexican noblewoman called 'Doña Marina', he set off to conquer Tenochtitlan.

An Aztec leader and members of his family shown in Aztec codex painting.

Moctezuma

The first meeting between Cortex and the Aztec leader, Moctezuma, was friendly. The Aztecs gave the Spaniards rich gifts to show that they were honoured guests. Moctezuma and Cortes spoke together with the help of Dona Marina, who acted as interpreter.

Dona Marina

Cortes

Aztec warrior

Spanish soldiers

After they reached Tenochtitlan, the Spaniards behaved badly. They imprisoned Moctezuma, and killed many Aztec nobles. Moctezuma tried to restore peace, but he too was killed when the citizens rioted.
The Spaniards tried to escape, but many were killed. Later they returned, and captured Tenochtitlan.

Spanish soldiers trapped inside Aztec palace

sword

angry Aztec guards

spear

shield

war club

padded cotton armour

Cortes the conqueror

Cortes had only 553 soldiers and 16 horses. But, by 1521, he had captured the city of Tenochtitlan, and overthrown the Aztec empire. How had this happened?

Partly, Moctezuma was defeated by his own fears. Today we know that the 'floating houses' and 'monsters' were only Cortes's sailing ships and men on horseback. But the Aztecs had not seen either of these things before, and were terrified. Partly, Aztec troops, although brave and well-trained, could not win against Spanish soldiers armed with guns and cross-bows. Most important of all, Cortes was helped by Mexican peoples conquered by the Aztecs, who disliked paying tribute, and hated seeing their men killed as sacrifices.

Spanish adventurers sailed in ships like these, shown on a 16th century Spanish tapestry. They were powered by the wind, caught in their vast sails.

What happened next?

Emperor Moctezuma was killed before Cortes conquered Tenochtitlan. Many Aztec nobles, and thousands of Aztec soldiers, died fighting to defend their land. But by 1535, the whole of Mexico was ruled by Spain.

Soon after, Spanish settlers arrived in Mexico. Like Cortes, they wanted wealth and power. They took over the best lands, and made the local people work for them. This was cruel and unjust, but the Mexican people were harmed even more by European diseases, especially measles and smallpox, brought by the settlers. Within 100 years, the population of the Aztec empire had fallen from about 11 million to only one million. Aztec power was gone forever.

Spanish coin, minted in the early 16th century. It is made of gold, and marked with a cross, the symbol of the Christian religion.

Soon after Cortes's victory, the Spanish king and queen sent missionary priests to Mexico to teach the Aztecs about the Christian faith. They tried to stop the worship of the old Aztec gods, pulled down the Aztec temples, and built new Christian churches and cathedrals in their place.

Since the 16th century, most people living in Mexico have been Christians.
But, many Aztec traditions, including the ancient Aztec language called Nahuatl, have survived until today.

Old Aztec priest.

Spanish cathedral next to the ruins of an Aztec temple in the centre of Tenochtitlan.

How do we know?

Many different types of evidence have survived to tell us about Aztec and Spanish people. How many examples have you spotted in this book?

There are surviving buildings, like the church opposite. There are carvings, like the stone calendar on page 20. There is pottery, like the little Aztec figure on page 6. There are wonderful mosaics, like the skull mask on page 12. Codexes (opposite), drawn by Aztec artists, record details of the Aztec way of life. Glittering coins (page 24) remind us of the Spanish quest for gold. And soldiers, missionaries and travellers have left us written descriptions of the time Aztecs and Spaniards came face to face.

Mask of the god Queztalcoatl. It is made of precious cedar wood, and decorated with turquoise chips.

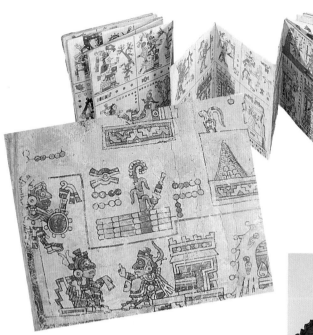

A complete codex. As you can see, these documents were made in long strips, and folded like a concertina, in zig-zags. Scribes used paper made from cactus fibre and paints made of coloured earths.

The great doorway of a Spanish church in Mexico city. It is built in a European, not an Aztec style, and decorated with scenes illustrating Christian beliefs.

A reconstruction, made by modern archaeologists, of the busy Aztec central market, held close to the city of Tenochtitlan. People came here from many parts of the Aztec empire, with food, clothes, jewels and all kinds of goods to sell. Reconstructions like this can help us understand what life was like in Aztec times.

Dates to remember

Aztecs

AD 1520
Moctezuma killed by angry Aztecs who think he has been friendly towards Cortes.

AD 1519
Moctezuma hears reports of strange 'monsters' arriving off Mexican coast.

AD 1427
Aztecs begin to fight neighbouring states to catch captives to sacrifice to their gods.

AD 1325
About now, the Aztecs begin to build their capital city of Tenochtitlan.

AD 1200-1300
Aztecs leave their original homeland and arrive in Mexico.

AD 2000

You were born

AD 1000

You were born

Spaniards

AD 1535
Spanish king sends governor to rule Mexico. First Spanish settlers arrive.

AD 1521
Cortes conquers the city of Tenochtitlan with the help of other Mexican peoples.

AD 1520
Cortes and his troops are driven out of Tenochtitlan by Aztecs. He seeks help from the Aztecs' enemies in Mexico.

AD 1519
Cortes arrives in Mexico.

AD 1494
Spain claims the right to conquer and rule large parts of the 'New World'—the lands visited by Spanish explorers.

AD 1492
The explorer Columbus, backed by Spain, crosses the Atlantic Ocean for the first time. He returns to Spain with stories about gold and treasures.

Words explained

Administrators People who organise and run governments and businesses.

Astronomers People who study the sun, moon, planets and stars.

Ceramic tiles Tiles made of clay, often decorated with brightly coloured pictures or patterns.

Codex A book written and illustrated by Aztec scribes, recording past happenings, stories, legends and religious beliefs. Some codexes also contain lists of tribute paid by conquered peoples, and details of everyday life.

Empire Land conquered and ruled by a stronger country.

Fertile Able to grow good crops.

Fibres Long, strong, string-like shreds which remain after the green fleshy part of a cactus leaf has rotted away.

Maize Sweetcorn.

Missionary Someone who travels to a distant land to teach people a new religious faith.

Mosaics Pictures made out of little pieces of glass or stone, carefully fitted together. The Aztecs covered the surface of some of their statues with mosaics.

Prophecy Words spoken by a religious leader (prophet), who believes that he or she has a message from the gods. Prophets sometimes claim to be able to tell what is going to happen in the future.

Reconstruction A model or a drawing made by historians and archaeologists based on evidence surviving from the past. Reconstructions are designed to help us understand what life was like in past times.

Scribes People who could read and write.

Tapestry A picture made by weaving different coloured threads together.

Tribute Payments, in money or goods, made by conquered peoples.